Amelie's 'Pebbles On The Shore'

An Oasis of Vivid hues

Dhanyashree B C

BookLeaf Publishing

India | USA | UK

Dedication

To the world of Poetry, My loved ones

&

Miraquill Poetry Forum

Preface

Poetry is the language of one's heart.
Years ago, a quiet whisper in me echoed with a passion
to be heard.
Which began the seeking of my inner world.
Words have the magic touch of a feather, and wings of
imagination to carry us to new dimensions.

It is with great pleasure, I share my thoughts with the
world through my lens, in this form.
This book in itself is a voyage to vivid realities of life.

Everything I am able to put forth here.. have blossomed,
just like a flower with all it's grace.

Acknowledgements

Many to acknowledge but this is dedicated to that one person,
who has been my roomie from mother's womb, my twin sister. Thank you for all the support.
My heartfelt gratitude to Miraquill for keeping the poet in me alive, showing me poetry in various forms & you really kept me going.

My family and friends have always been a source of encouragement & motivation.
Many thanks to them.

Sincere thanks to my readers

Life

I boarded the ship of Life,
Sailing in the sea of hope..
I have to face the tides,
In order to reach the shore.
The tides are striking me,
I shall never bother..
For my aim is to reach the shore,
Before I go to..,
Endless sleep..!

Earthling's love

We call it Home,
A place inhabited by civilizations..
The warmth in this soil,
says, I know this place so well.

Across Lightyears and Centuries,
From Dinosaurs to Human kind..
Stone age to Modern Age..
A place like no other..

Every time you embraced..
In all the various forms that I have come in here,
How can one carry all the pain,
and be so dear..

All I can say,
I left my footprints on the shore..
To comeback for more & more..
So as to rewrite my story in a better way.

Give me your patience,
your resilience..
I have only taken from You..
My hands are full, while I was emptying you..

I look out for a way,
To see you rejoice..
A day that's not far away,
For us to make the right choice..
Time to hear your voice,
Would you let us all stay?

Rooted

I dance to the tunes of singing breeze,
Chained are my roots to mother earth..
And in winters I begin to freeze,
I protect you in every birth.

And my love for you will never cease,
For my every breath is of worth..
In autumns I shed my leaves with ease,
I'm home to hear the sweet bird's mirth.

I dance to the tunes of singing breeze,
Chained are my roots to mother earth..
And in winters I begin to freeze,
I protect you in every birth.

Let Go

I thought always, it was mine..
Holding on to it was just fine.
When things turned out new,
I was left with few..
There was a bird caged so long,
That had to fly & sing it's own song.

The trees shed their leaves,
The clouds shower the rain,
The river flows endlessly,
Well it does all of this effortlessly.

Starting to look at nature,
The closed doors of my heart, opened.
I had in me, some things to nurture,
I was awakened.

Let it Go, You feel so light..
If it's meant for you, It never looses it's sight.

Dancing to Glory

Time to fly, let your wings not rest..
You've chosen to let go off your nest.
Remember where you'd collapsed,
To rise beyond it with glory..

Keep your roots firm,
They shall always stand by
In Tides & Winds,
To sustain when tough times pass by.

What is that you've got,
Have your purpose in sight.
Keep going,
In order to find your way.

Failures come to strengthen you,
Let it empower you.

In all his plan my dear,
He was beside you..

Showing that the dark clouds
shall pass, Don't miss your view.

Only then you are reborn,
To write all your victorious tomorrows.

Broken is Beautiful

In Life, everything breaks!
Trust, Friendships,
Relationships, Love,
Compassion, Hope, Passion,
All this happens in this tiny little 'Heart'.

The true beauty is, we gather unknowingly..
Those broken pieces and join them together,
To complete the amazing Puzzle of Life.

Don't fret or fear.
You can fix the things that's broken.
We break terribly,
innumerable times..
Yet, God reshapes us lovingly!

Merry-Me-In

An
Array
Of tunes
In this heart

Lingers as I gaze
At the horizon of my dreams

There is no limit, you have the power to unleash
Whispers my soul with ease and says live every moment
there lies your true potential

What if the universe granted your every wish, that
brings you closer to the fulfillment you seek

Some days are sunny, others may rain, Find your true
solace that fills you with utmost joy.
In solitude can you find the deeper meanings of life and
in silence your calm,

In the end all that matters is
How you lived and led.
What you gave,
All for a
Good
Sake

Lighthouse

When the meandering waves,
make their own sound..
I sail with it..
hearing the waves rebound.

The calm ocean,
filled with life deep within..
No roar, no scream,
ripples of calm on the brim.

When the waves
knock the shore with joy..
and go back they show
How to let go
no hurry no cry..

Sometimes the wind
Change the course..
When in life's crossroads,
Where does it take you further..

No one knows..

As the dusk unfolds,
On the vast sky's canvas..,
Isn't it incredible?
To witness what it holds..

Some~Say

Somewhere in those doors,
Were the keys hidden.
Somehow the earth,
Recovers its losses.

Someday we all hope,
Is going to be the best day of our lives.
Someone unknown,
Helps you in need.

Something you hid,
To surprise your loved one.
Somebody shared with you,
A secret to keep.

Someway life answers,
Your deepest prayers.
Sometimes what lies ahead,
Is already within.

In the Dawn

Here comes the light
Bigger and bright
Tell me what tore you apart..
Let it faint..
You played your part..

Here comes the light
Magnificent like the knight..
Let the stories of your struggles,
Lead you to an astounding path..

Here comes the light
As a beacon of hope..
Let nothing stop you,
Have your eyes on the goal..

Here comes the light
Like never before..
Gather your courage..

Take a big leap..
You are capable of more..

15

Oh My Heart

You keep running like in a marathon..
Amidst all that's going on,
I wish to applaud, to cheer
For not letting me stop
Be it Sunshine or dark..

There were days and
Times when I fell apart..
You stood with me,
Silently sobbing,
Still fueling me from inside.

You are me and I am you.
Which is why..
I can't fly without you..
You know all of my weakness
And strengths to push through..

Give me another chance,
Let your head be held high..

Nothing is out of reach,
Until we made our mind..
Give me passion to pursue, this time..

The Storyteller

A tale
That never ends..
Crafted in solitude
What life sends..

Diving deep into the unknown,
Flying across the vast sky..
Like a universe of her own.

When the heart's deep feelings,
Like watercolors
Fill the canvas of imagination
To take their own shape..
A story is born..

In the valley of words,
A race of space..
Empty pages,
Embracing them with grace.

Pauses and Scribbles..
Stammers and slows,
However the suspense..
Magically unfolds.

And when it's bedtime for kids,
Comforting
Like a pillow,
To put them to sleep..

It reminds me of my grandmother,
With endless fables to tell..
Even today in my memories,
They surely and dearly dwell.

An Ode of Zest

A deep calling
Beyond the limiting beliefs
Constantly lights in the heart.
Dreams appear of it,
Existing in a parallel universe.
Fervently reminding,
Giving up is easy..
Holding on to
Instincts in this limited time,
Journeying with it,
Keeps you awake.
Let your passion blossom,
Mold it every single day.
Nightmares don't last long,
Only your undivided attention,
Paves way for new possibilities.
Questions may arise.
Reflections of your experiences,
Serve as a guiding light.
Time for you to decide,

Undoubtful of what lies around the corner.

Visit the truths..

Warriors are undefeated..

Xerically adapted like the cactus in a desert,

Your have that

Zeal.

Vibes of Bliss

When the golden rays of the sun..
Touch the waves of the ocean,
Dancing with the wind..
A beautiful escape into a world unknown,
My eyes takes in so much light..
Like a diamond's luster,
Brilliant and bright..

The water seems sparkling..
With love and hope..
The sands on the shore,
Holds so many things dear..
A name, a castle, countless footprints..
Giving all it away, back to the ocean..
Waiting what every tomorrow brings..

The sight of faraway sailing ships..
Like a parade,
That has already passed our way.

The view of the horizon..
Like a simply drawn line,
My eyes can't stop looking out..
At such an astounding sight.

Among all of them..
Those who live in,
These lovely acrobats..
Never fail to amuse
While the sun begins to set..
Closing the day..

Light in the Dark

In tough times..
Let strength come to you.
When you think you're drowning..
Let courage find you.

In times when you know,
You have fought enough battles..
Why don't you rest..
Yes it may seem the end,
Don't you think it's a new beginning?

Life knocks you,
Puts you down..
After all the storms don't last a lifetime..
It's you, who can change the course.
When the winds of change..
Begin to pull you aside,
Take your path and set your sail.

When all you believed,

Begins to shatter..
Its for you to get better.

Do carry
Efforts that
Shaped you.
Time
Is
Not stopping
You.

The Unexplored Diary

Years gone by..
Stories untold..
As I step by..
On a treasure unexplored..

A blanket of webs..
Dust it sheds..

As curiosity awaits..
My hands begin to shake,
To hold something lost,
May be dear to someone
That rests..

A lost throne..
Or a memoir,
A long kept secret..
Or a heart so lone yet dear..

What could be this,

Lying so long unknown...
Lost with time..
With some pages torn

A mystery..
I stumbled upon,
I begin to explore..
It's lonely song...

Words faded,
Leading to a heart's play..
Opening new doors...
Showing another gateway..

I begin to wonder,
To whom it belongs..
As it unfolds to me..
As a beautiful song..

On a winter evening..
It haunts me,
To bring it back to life..
My hands get wiped with a shade of hope
That it tried to find itself,
In the mines of darkness..

I am quite sure,

It stood the test of time, undoubted..
Unknown for what it was bound..

Journey to Truth

When the gushing winds
Pass through my ears,
Overpouring thoughts,
Finding to make its way..

I stood there like a flickering light,
Wondering what shook me..
I found no answer anyway.
Sure something had changed,
That caught my sight.

The rumbling leaves
Disperse gently
Twirling in the air..
Falling merrily..

And now my mind
Dwindling into silence..
Feels like the ocean breeze
Calm and clear..

Embracing peace.

Shimmering ocean waters..
With the setting sun..
Holds me tight..
In the moment to stay.

Letter to a Friend

As I walk past that bridge..
Where we once crossed,
The doors of the passed days,
No longer wish to stay close..
They sway and say..

It's been a long time,
That we walked together..
Had so much to talk.
Tirelessly all through the night.

I wish you were beside,
On those happiest days,
Also when I went totally mad..
When my breath got heavy,
As I sat in silence all along.

You're that One..
This heart feels close,
Despite being miles apart.

I constantly remember
The times we spent
Forever to cherish..
That I dearly kept.

A Rainbow Dream

I sat on a lovely wooden bench,
Painted beautifully Violet..
Spotting the Indigo bunting..
Gazing at the Blue sky.

The light Green leaves on the tree so fresh & bright..
There is a bumblebee collecting Yellow nectar,
On those Orange honey suckle flowers..
As I watch nature unfold in it's own way, the sky turns
Red..
Looks like it's time for the sun, to put an end to the day..

With my eyes calmed,
I go to sleep ..
To relive this Rainbow dream.

Tranquil

The golden gates of time..
I watch like a gatekeeper,
Patiently for that moment..
Which makes my heart fly
Across the beautiful sky
Beyond the reach of my hands.
I wish to be still in that moment..
Then my heart drifts back slowly..
Like a feather,
And rests finally in peace.
On the divine soil
Where I once engraved
My identity

The broken walls of the past
Do not bother me anymore
All of which i left there
Has either been burried
Or has vanished over time.

This last breath
How would it be?
Who knows..
Forever the soul
Finally has found its way back home.
A story that god wrote
For each one of us
On his own.

Nature's Symphony

When the fog engulfs..
the morning sky,
I looked for the Sun,
Hoping he would show up..
To say hello & pass by.

The clock struck twelve..
Why the day is so dull..
Just then the cold winds,
come dancing by.

As time runs..
and the mist disappears,
That's when his glory,
brightens the day..
Life renews in it's own
beautiful way.

Lush green leaves and
the budding flowers' scent..

Birds chirping with merry..
A treat to the eyes,
A day well spent.

As days begin to unwind,
The scorching rays appear..
when the hot breeze,
hits my face..
and the days turn longer,
I wish to rest.

When the dark clouds,
bring some hope..
I look at them as they gather,
wanting the rains to shower..

As I hear the clattering sound,
of the first drop that hits the ground,
my heart is filled with joy..
A welcome song of the monsoon.

Happy streams and gushing rivers..
Roaring ocean waves..
Merry is in the air.
quenching all the thirst..
Soon the pages turn,
and the leaves turn brown..

Red and yellow..
bright orange everywhere..
A beautiful Potrait..
I wonder who's painted..
distinctly decorating,
the earth charming
gracefully..